Enneagram exercises for personal growth

Enneagram Type 4
The Individualist

Created by Youaremoreworld

Enneagram exercises for personal growth: The Individualist
Created by Youaremoreworld

Copyright ©Youaremoreworld

For more information visit us: www.youaremoreworld.com or contact via email:
youaremoreworld@gmail.com

The names of the people in this book have been changed in order to protect their privacy.

The text was written by Viltare Veckyte based on the knowledge of Enneagram.

Graphics designed by: Simona Pozyte

First printed on Amazon, 2021.

ISBN 9798550352250

I welcome you
on the journey of
self discovery

agree to do daily exercises which will lead me to my personal growth. I do this because I see the importance of releasing my old habits and taking full responsibility for creating the life I want to live. I want to grow and explore my potential.

I will be true to myself by following daily practices which will encourage self-empowerment and personal appreciation. From today onward, personal growth will be one of my highest priorities in every day, and I promise to spend at least 10 minutes a day doing something which supports my true self.

_____   _____
Signature   Date

Introduction

Dear reader,

This Enneagram exercise book is a valuable tool which can guide you along your spiritual journey, helping you to grow and expand to your true nature. The material is intended to support those who already have some understanding of the Enneagram and are most likely also familiar with their own personality type. It will support these readers to go deeper by unraveling behavioural patterns and releasing blocks which may be preventing them from experiencing their full potential.

If you are unfamiliar with Enneagram and uncertain of your Enneagram type, a great place to start is to take an Enneagram Personality Test. This test along with other helpful information can be found at **www.youaremoreworld.com**.

The book opens with a foreword from the author, as she addresses all those who share your type, reminding you that you are not alone in the concerns which you experience. In the following pages you will be guided to discover more about your type from the basis of the behavioral patterns which are common for your personality type; exploring what you like, what is important to you and also what is essential in order for you to maintain balance in your day-to-day life. There are many thoughts which are valuable for you to bring awareness to which can help you to find greater connection with yourself.

The introductory Enneagram theory was left out of this book, as there are many valuable and in-depth sources where this can be explored. The aim of this book is to bring a fresh perspective to Enneagram, through working with habitual personality patterns, discovering greater understanding of personality traits and releasing false stories through daily practices. The resulting goal is to support you in your daily experiences and to guide you into the full integration of you with your wholeness. Within this book you will find some daily practices from well know Enneagram teachers, as well as practices which have been tailored specifically for your personality type. By applying these practices daily you will experience the greatest benefit, gaining a better understanding of yourself, your preferences and your relationships. Through this work on the exercises you will experience the freedom which has always been a part of you, increasing your self-esteem and unraveling your unique gifts and strengths.

This book offers you the path to the truth which will free you to your wholeness.

Author's note

Thank you for trusting in me to guide you to explore your inner world.

We could all agree that life can be considered a journey, filled with ups and downs; joys and sadness. All of these moments arrive and then fade away, and all the while we remain observers to the experience simply noticing these changes as they occur. As we travel on this journey, we all reach moments when we begin to question ourselves, looking for new ways to change the course of our lives. In moments like these we are drawn to look within our own hearts and truly meet ourselves, sometimes for the very first time.

This Enneagram exercise book was created for this purpose of discovering greater inner awareness, offering guidance for you who have recognised that you hold dominant qualities of "The Individualist". It will support you and remind you that you are not alone on this journey; that many of us have similar questions and are also seeking a deeper connection to ourselves.

This book will also provide a blueprint for greater personal understanding and the support to unfold all of the qualities which you hold within, to truly flourish within your experience of life. It will remind you that there is no better path to personal growth than simply laying out all of our qualities in plain sight; seeing them as they are and recognising the value that each one of them brings us.

The information contained within this book can hold tremendous power for personal change and by exploring this book you may also experience some changes within yourself. When faced with this new information and the resulting changes, your willingness to remain open can allow you to discover more about yourself, and your experience of life, than you might expect.

As you turn the page you will be taking your first step on this new journey.

Are you ready?

How to use this book

This book is made up of four parts: Discovering Myself, Revealing Myself, Accepting Myself and Healing Myself. Although it can be tempting to skip ahead, we recommend using this book in the order in which it is laid out, as each chapter can provide a greater depth of understanding and when followed as recommended, has the potential to create powerful changes in your life.

Chapter   – **"Discovering Myself"** – This chapter explores many aspects of your dominant type, bringing you greater awareness of your personal traits. This exploration allows you to determine if this is truly your dominant type and to see yourself from an open and understanding perspective, to better understand the basis of this dominant Enneagram type. You will also learn to recognize your personal traits, your gifts and the challenges you face related to having this dominant type.

Chapter   – **"Revealing Myself"** – This chapter leads you through 40 exercises which have been created specifically for your dominant type. These exercises will expand your understanding of situations you face and also awaken a deeper connection with yourself through awareness of your daily behaviors. It is very important that you complete each of the exercises as they each have a meaningful message which can only be explored through personal experience. You will find that there is also great value in writing your thoughts and observations as well as the feelings you experience as you go, as this can develop a deeper connection within yourself.

Chapter   – **"Accepting Myself"** – This chapter will provide you with a greater sense of acceptance of who you are. Having explored the dominant qualities of your Enneagram type and some of the repetitive situations you find yourself falling into, you might begin to feel more aware of who you are in the present moment. You may still feel some hesitation about some of your qualities, but allowing yourself to practice acceptance of who you are in this moment will allow you to experience a greater sense of freedom of who you can be. You will discover how you can apply this self-acceptance to your own life. Only when we accept the qualities, we do not like about ourselves do we gain the freedom to choose how we really want to be.

Chapter   – **"Healing Myself"** – Each of us has many qualities that were formed in order to protect us. As we grow and develop, we begin to recognize some of them as qualities we do not really like but we feel powerless to change them. First, through our awareness we can notice them, then through acceptance we bring them out of the shadows, and finally through healing we can lovingly change and release them. In this section you will find carefully selected practices that can help you to observe and connect with these qualities in greater depth, which when practiced daily, can cause a very big shift in your life.

Discovering myself

Insightful questionnaire

Type description

Childhood message

How to get along with you

Famous people who share your type

Personal stories shared by others of your type

Before we start, mark the qualities that resonate with you

This section was created to determine whether this workbook is best suited to your dominant Enneagram type.

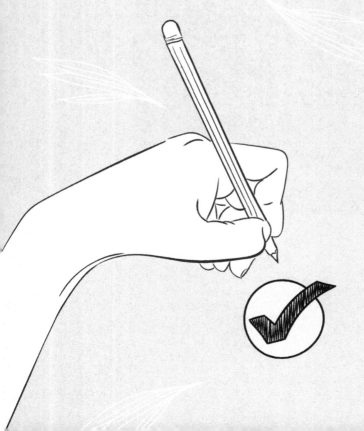

☑ I want to feel **unique and original;**

☑ I am **sensitive and empathetic;**

◯ I often feel **lonely** even when I am surrounded by people;

☑ For me, the most important thing in life is **love;**

☑ I don't like when **others tell me what I should do,** for some reason it

　　encourages me to do the opposite;

☑ I spend a lot of time **imagining conversations** that won't necessarily happen

　　in the future;

☑ I feel that **others do not understand me;**

☑ I feel **different** from those around me;

☑ I like to decorate my environment, gather interesting and original details

　　for the house;

◯ I feel like something is always **missing,** but it is hard to put in words what it is;

◯ I often **focus on the past** and long for it;

☑ I'm always looking for something **unique, original, deep, exciting in life;**

☑ I am very sensitive to **beauty, love, sadness and pain;**

◯ I am **introverted;**

◯ I often **feel misunderstood**, which encourages me to distance myself

　　from other people;

☑ I am **romantic;**

◯ I seek a **close relationship**, it is important for me to understand the other

　　person's feelings;

◯ I admire people with qualities I don't have. I envy them and inside I

　　underestimate myself thinking that something is wrong with me;

◯ I often hear a voice inside saying, "you will fail" or "you are worthless";

　　I admit, I often feel dissatisfied with myself;

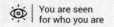
○ It is sometimes difficult for me to put thoughts into fluent sentences, so I
am **often silent** when I am in a large group of people;

○ People often find me **weird;**

✓ I judge other people if they do not stand out for their uniqueness or
peculiar style;

○ I love **sincerity and truth,** so I always say what I think, and I expect the
same from the others, even if the truth sometimes hurts;

○ I don't like to talk about boring everyday topics;

✓ My **mood changes very often and it has a big impact** on my level of energy
and decisions I make;

○ I like to **work alone,** it is important for me that the work is done the way I want;

✓ I always think about how to make my work **original and exclusive;**

○ I like to **improve everything around** me because I easily notice if something
is missing;

✓ I am **creative** and I have a vivid imagination;

○ I **prefer to listen** than to talk about myself;

✓ I like to **dive deep** into my inner world, **analyze** feelings and experiences and
look for the meaning of life;

✓ I feel alive when my life is filled with **intense emotions;**

✓ People who are able to be open and express all of their emotions seem
strong to me;

✓ I value **sincerity, depth and freedom** because these are my core values,
this is me;

✓ I can be **critical** and demand that people meet the standards I have set.

MY RESULT:

 *20* /**35**

If you ticked **more than 25 out of 35,** you are most likely a
Type 4 — also called "The Individualist" — and we welcome you to
continue your journey. In the following pages you will discover a
deeper understanding of yourself along with the tools and support
you need to experience your inner authenticity.

If you ticked **fewer than 25,** we recommend that you read more
about Types 1, 2, 5 and 9, which are the most common mistyped
personalities for Type 4.

The
INDI VIDUA LIST

They are one of the most **empathic** and **authentic** of all types, who are also especially intuitive and sensitive people, often following their hearts. They are **idealists,** deeply experiencing the whole spectrum of emotions, their mood can constantly change, often leading to dramatic bursts of emotions which can push others away.

The desire to be unique makes The INDIVIDUALIST **very creative.** They often choose a profession that is related to art. From early on they already see themselves as **different from other people.** They feel like **no one can understand them** or is capable to love them as they are able to love. Their focus is often on the things which separate them from others, which leads to the feeling that something is missing but difficult to put into words what exactly that is.

Your true nature:

To forgive and allow life experiences to change you.

The most important mission for me is to **find my own identity** and **personal worth.**

Even if people of this type feel that they are different, they do not want to be alone. From the outside, they might appear to be shy or even arrogant and to push others away, but deep inside **they want to connect with others and understand them.**

They are known as **Romantics** in Enneagram, waiting until someone evaluates the mystery of their personality and their capability to hide from the world: **"No one understands me, I am different and unique."** Freedom is very important as they do not like to be restrained and follow the rules of society. Somehow, they always have to **do things in their own way.** People of this type tend to see themselves from a negative perspective, constantly comparing themselves with others and feeling undervalued. Thinking that something is wrong with them, they do not have access to their good qualities. They grow by understanding that a lot of **stories in their heads are not true** or that they are no longer true. The majority of the time they create their own image of themselves in their head instead of trying to embrace their qualities and talents in reality. The biggest challenge for them is to let go of the memories of the past, they tend to keep negative feelings towards those who have hurt them.

Type fours identify with their own feelings „I am what I feel". They always look for intense emotions in their work and relationships. The stronger the emotions, the more alive they feel. There is a fear that if they won't experience any emotions, their creativity and personality will disappear.

By developing their personality, type fours begin to experience a fuller sense of themselves. They discover that **they are in fact as good as everyone else**, embracing their body as beautiful, recognizing their own uniqueness and **finding the love** that they were always seeking, **within their own heart.** This expanded love for themselves allows them to recognize how many good qualities they have, fostering their **self-esteem** and a **genuine sense of their own identity.** They experience inner contentment and no longer seek love from outside themselves, rather feeling drawn to **work toward the good of others** and to **find connection to the people around them.**

Your growth begins...

when you start **feeling unity** with the world and **appreciate being here** and now in the moment; when you feel your body and the processes happening inside. **Accept yourself as you are,** without thinking about the need to be exceptional and unique. Feel happiness, when you're experiencing unity with everyone in this world. Understand that constant suffering and inner fantasies are not necessary and lead you deeper in your unhealthy behavior patterns. **Harmony and wholeness** come from learning to accept your true self.

I see you

What is important to you:

Uniqueness
Feelings
A need to be different
Creativity
Meaningful experiences
Be true to yourself

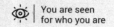

You do not feel good:

When you don't feel
personal worth.

You believe:

That you need to be unique and
you can't be happy and
live well in this world.

It is important to you:

To feel unique and
different from the others and
experience intense feelings.

I wish for you:

To accept yourself and value
people around you.

What I like
about my type:

- ◈ Ability to find **meaning in life;**
- ◈ Ability to **experience** all **feelings deeply;**
- ◈ Ability to **build deep relationships** with people who are important to me through empathy and support for those in difficult situations;
- ◈ **Creativity, intuition** and a **sense of aesthetics;**
- ◈ Being **authentic** to myself and others.

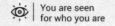
The Message from Childhood

The knowledge of Enneagram gives us an explanation of how our personalities have been formed. This formation starts from a very early age and in Enneagram is referred to as **"the message we received in childhood"**.

We came into this world to express our full potential. In the first stages of our life, we do not have any personal conclusions about the world, for example what is „good" or what is „bad". From the moment we are born our mind is already actively observing our surroundings and with every interaction it forms an understanding of the world. During this very vulnerable stage of our development **our parents play a significant role.** We are instinctively wired for belonging to them and they become our whole world during this period of life. As we observe their behavior and day-to-day responses, we form our understanding of the world around us.

However, at this stage we do not have much experience with which to compare and we collect many false messages, conclusions which might be reached from having just one bad experience. For example: your parents may not have wanted to play with you and did not explain why, so you might have come to your own conclusion about why they do not want to play with you. Or perhaps you were in the hospital and your mother could not come to visit you on time because of problems at her work and you might have come to the conclusion that you need to take care of yourself because no one else will. **Take a good look at the messages** written on the following page, **allow yourself to stay with them** observing what they bring to you. If it is difficult for you to find meaning in the messages this is totally natural, simply take further steps to explore more about your type and occasionally return to these messages to see if they bring more meaning to you.

Misunderstood message

The message we received in childhood and understood as truth, basing our further life experience on.

**"It is not okay to function well
or to be happy."**

Core fear

The inner fear that triggers us to build certain qualities in order to protect ourselves.

"I am afraid to be without identity or personal significance."

Lost message

The supportive message we were craving from others, but never received.

**"It is not true -
you are seen for who you are."**

21

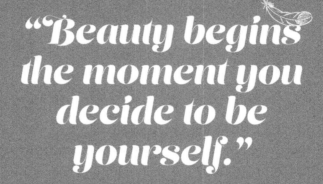

"Beauty begins the moment you decide to be yourself."

Coco Chanel

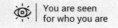
What other people of your type say about themselves

Enneagram knowledge helps us to see that some of our behavioral patterns, preferences and views about the world are shared with others who belong to the same dominant Enneagram type as us. This can give us comfort in the knowledge that we are not alone on this journey and we can always find someone who understands us in greater depth. Take a good look at the following sentences shared by people of your type.

◈ It is important for me to be **original.**

◈ I often notice how I can be overcome by **nostalgia,** opting to stay in that feeling rather than really experiencing the life that is happening right in front of me.

◈ I am always on a journey to **discover who I am.**

◈ I **undervalue others** if they do not stand out with their uniqueness.

◈ I am always hoping to find the one who will actually **see who I truly am.**

◈ I can realize myself through the **love I give to other people.**

◈ I tend to play a **game of 'hide-and-seek',** to see if those that I care about truly love me.

◈ My **fantasy world** is so powerful that it can take over the majority of my life.

◈ I look for ways to **experience emotions** so that I can feel more alive.

◈ It is **hard for me to forgive** to those who hurt my feelings.

How to get along with me

We can build deeper understanding in our relationships by sharing what is important to us. Through sharing our preferences, others will understand us more intimately, often resulting in them offering greater support to us. In turn this gives us more opportunities to offer the same support to others.

Below are some key qualities which, when respected, provide those of our type a supportive basis to be the best they can be.

1. Give me some compliments. It is very important for me.

2. Be supportive. Help me to love and value myself.

3. Value my intuition and imagination.

4. Never say that I am too emotional or that I exaggerate situations.

5. Help me to see my uniqueness in simply being who I am.

6. Encourage me to take action.

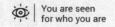
Famous people like you

The best teachers are the ones who have walked a similar path ahead of us. Their examples can give us hope, inspiration and guidance on where we can take our own paths and how our qualities can empower us on this journey.

The Enneagram Institute has compiled a very comprehensive list of well-known people who share the same dominant Enneagram type as you. Take some time to explore the lives of the people listed below and you may discover what a valuable resource it can be for your own development.

Rumi, Frédéric Chopin, Pyotr I. Tchaikovsky, Gustav Mahler, Jackie Kennedy Onassis, Edgar Allen Poe, Yukio Mishima, Virginia Woolf, Anne Frank, Karen Blixen / Isak Dinesen, Anaïs Nin, Tennessee Williams, J.D. Salinger, Anne Rice, Frida Kahlo, Diane Arbus, Martha Graham, Rudolf Nureyev, Cindy Sherman, Hank Williams, Billie Holiday, Judy Garland, Maria Callas, Miles Davis, Keith Jarrett, Joni Mitchell, Bob Dylan, Paul Simon, Leonard Cohen, Yusuf Islam (Cat Stevens), Ferron, Cher, Stevie Nicks, Annie Lennox, Prince, Sarah McLachlan, Alanis Morrisette, Feist, Florence (+ the Machine) Welch, Amy Winehouse, Ingmar Bergman, Lars von Trier, Marlon Brando, Jeremy Irons, Angelina Jolie, Winona Ryder, Kate Winslet, Nicolas Cage, Johnny Depp, Tattoo Artist Kat Von D., Magician Criss Angel, Streetcar Named Desire's "Blanche duBois"

(Source: www.enneagraminstitute.com)

Nothing is absolute.
Everything changes,
everything moves,
everything revolves,
everything flies
and goes away.

Frida Kahlo

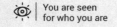
At your best you
open up and become:

Expressive Intuitive
Self- disciplined
Compassionate
Authentic
Creative

When you do not feel balanced
you tend to:

Jealous Depressive
Temperamental
Self-Absorbed
Unproductive
Critical

People of your type shared some stories from their life

It is crucial for me to understand who I am and why I am who I am. I searched for information, did personality tests, and read books about personalities, looking for ways to describe myself. It seemed that when I would find myself, everything would fall into place. But now, 15 years on, I am still looking for myself and I think the process will not end there. I have realized that every experience I have changes me as a person and it brings even greater joy when I don't focus so strongly on myself but try to connect to other people more.

— Wayne, 39.

I had a big idea a few years ago. As soon as it was time to do something in order to realize it, it was hard to bring myself to act, instead I would turn on movies and watch them without stopping or just sleep all day until I completely forgot who and where I was. I allowed myself to do everything except the things which needed to be done, simply following my desires. But then I felt very bad, disgusted with myself, and blamed myself for not being able to finish anything. I thought I was wasting my life and achieving nothing. I would stay in that state for days, sometimes even reaching a state of depression and apathy to life.

— Suzanne, 26.

I often felt out of touch with my environment. I thought that those around me didn't understand me, and I saw myself as if I was from another world. I really wanted to be invited to parties, but when I did go I faced the same problem every time - I thought I didn't have anything interesting to say which only made me stay in silence. When I would return home, I felt disappointed that again I wasn't able to reveal myself, to be like the others, to joke and talk about nothing. A part of me wanted to feel like a normal person as those around me did, but at the same time I appreciated that I was different, more mature and seeing the world in a deeper way than others. I have noticed that after learning to push away my belief that I can't and don't want to talk about simple topics like the weather, I have met many amazing people, because in the end it's not important how the conversation starts, what's more important is where it can take you and you have the power to give your input on where it goes. It's important to simply communicate and find a connection!

- Laura, 31.

People often say to me that I look sad. Sometimes I feel an inexplicable need to experience sadness, even if there is no reason. Those around me try to entertain me, but they don't realize that I like sadness, it helps me to understand myself better. I become stronger and besides, sadness ends at some point and then I realize new things about myself as a result. How can one see the meaning of light without seeing darkness?

– Thomas, 29.

At work, it is very important to me that my colleagues and manager evaluate my ideas as original and unique. I try to create in ways which are meaningful to me, I avoid rules created by other people and their imposed opinions. I'm always looking for ways to make my work different. I even find it hard to send it to clients if the work doesn't look original enough. I keep finding flaws, looking for something else to improve, sometimes it takes a while and I can even miss the deadline. I'm afraid that if I send out uninteresting work, those around me will think I'm uninteresting, too.

- Ray, 42.

"

I've always loved solitude, I enjoy it. Although some people find this abnormal, when I no longer try to deny this part of myself I more and more frequently spend time with others, but only with those with who I feel good, where it is not necessary to fill the silence with meaningless chatter about nothing. Being with people gives me energy, especially, when we're discussing spiritual and deep topics, then I feel like there is not enough time in the day, and we can talk for hours. There are only a couple of people with who I talk to about everything and I can freely express what I think.

— Dan, 47.

"

It's extremely hard for me to let go of the past, I often long for what was. I remember all of the insults or criticisms, and it's hard for me to forgive people who insulted or rejected me. When these thoughts flood in I can spend the whole day examining who said or did what and relive the anger and all of the emotions. I usually remember the moments which stir up the most emotions, I repeat them over and over again in my head. I have always been very sensitive to my surroundings and have taken the words and criticisms which people said very personally. I often push away or ignore the people who hurt my feelings, they become worthless to me. I don't want to be like that anymore, now I'm trying to let go of the past and live more in the present.

— George, 34.

It always seemed to me that people didn't see the real me. I have a vision of what I would like to be. I create all of the qualities I want, but I often find that I don't do anything to develop them. It still seems like now is the wrong time, something is still missing for me to achieve my dreams. I can spend all day watching TV series or movies, empathizing with the lives of others, experiencing all of the emotions of the characters and forgetting myself. Reality doesn't seem to exist for me. Time is running out, I live in fantasies and I realize I'm just postponing my life. I have learned to accept myself as I am now, with all of the qualities I have. I am practising seeing the positive side rather than always focusing on what I don't have. If I really feel like I want to develop new qualities, I set up a realistic plan of how to do it.

— Edith, 51.

> *I kept getting involved in relationships with foreigners who lived far away from me. I didn't notice how I became trapped in my fantasies, after all I could imagine the relationship in any way I wanted. Through the days I would dream of myself and my partner, thinking about how we would spend our time, communicating and creating all of the details of our future meetings. Often those fantasies became so twisted that I would lose sight of reality. I would become so infatuated, not with the real person, but with the kind of person I created in my head. When we met, most of details I had imagined didn't come true and I felt frustrated with both myself and that person. I knew I had wasted those months and did not see the true reality. I realize now that I was really attached to the idea of unreachability and longing which was easy to maintain when forming a relationship with a person living far away.*
>
> *— Grace, 27.*

> *When I have to make a decision, I analyze all of the circumstances, but in the end I always make the final decision only by listening to my heart. I am very intuitive, sometimes I just know. I don't know how, but I often see what will happen before it does or how a person is going to feel about a given situation. Over time I have learned to listen to that feeling because it is always right. The feeling can show up in the middle of the night or simply by looking at a person. In situations like this, I am able to leave doubts behind, even if intuition says the opposite of what I expected or would have liked. This feeling has always helped me to choose paths in situations where I can't see the solution only with my mind.*
>
> *— Sharla, 43.*

Revealing myself

Tips for personal awareness

Thoughts encouraging growth

40 daily exercises

Bringing awareness to yourself

By becoming aware of your day-to-day behavior, you gain the ability to respond to situations in the way that you truly want to. Take a good look at the following recommendations which were created specifically for your type. Expand your awareness by integrating them into your daily practices.

◈ **Practice** acceptance that you are not your feelings. Your feelings reveal only the current situation, not more.

◈ **Write down** your talents and evaluate them. Notice your belief that some people are better than you, question if this is really true.

◈ **Observe your tendency** to maintain a state of sadness that sets you apart from other people. Understand that even if you are happy you will remain unique.

◈ **Notice that when you focus on what is missing, you lose the opportunity to enjoy what is happening in your life right now.**

◈ **Practice** catching yourself when you wander into the past. Bring yourself back to the present. Notice the good things which are in your life in this present moment.

◈ **Notice** when you disappear and "hide", waiting for others to see that.

◈ **Observe yourself when you make negative comparisons.**

◈ **Notice** when you see others as better people who have qualities you are missing.

◈ **Choose** a form of exercise you like and practice it regularly. This will help you to feel more grounded and connected with reality.

- It is important to realize that anything can be interesting. What is happening here and now is just as valuable as what you are missing at the moment. Maybe there is no need to suffer or detach, just accept the moment as it is.

- **Notice** when you create conversations in your head in everyday situations about what you could have done differently.

- **Practice** releasing painful moments from the past. Notice how they interfere with living in the present.

- **Do not delay** your plans just because you expect to be in the right mood later.

- **Notice** that by caring what other people think of you, you do not allow yourself to stay **true in the moment** and **fully express yourself.**

- **Practice acceptance** that to experience the fullness of all emotions, they do not have to be intense or dramatized.

- **Be aware when you see yourself pushing to be unique instead of seeing yourself as unique in this present moment for who you are already.**

- **Notice** when you intentionally create drama in order to intensify your relationships.

- **Take time** for practices that awaken inner love for yourself, reducing overemphasis. Love and feel compassion toward yourself.

- **Practice forgiveness** and use your life experience for personal growth and change.

- **Bring awareness** to seeing yourself as an important and interesting person as everybody else is.

Thoughts
Encouraging Growth

Every thought has the potential to take your life in a new direction. The following messages were carefully selected for your Enneagram type. Take some time to read each message and consider how you can incorporate them into your daily life.

- You are **already unique**, you don't have to try to be even more that way. You are already like no other person on this planet.

- Your spiritual growth begins when you **free yourself from the past** and **allow yourself to be naturally changed** by life experiences flowing through you.

- Set your own personal agenda, **don't wait for creative inspiration** to come. Even a small plan can motivate you to take action.

- Notice when too much **concentration on yourself** reduces empathy for others.

- **Notice** when you start pushing others away.

- **Grow the understanding** that wholeness exists in the present. Be here and now, feel the moment without letting yourself move into the emotions of the past.

- Emotional instability and bad mood are not the same as **emotional sensitivity.**

- People see you as who you are already, you do not need to try to be **unique.**

- **Practice gratitude** for things you already have.

- When we spend moments in our **imaginary world,** we steal them from our daily real life.

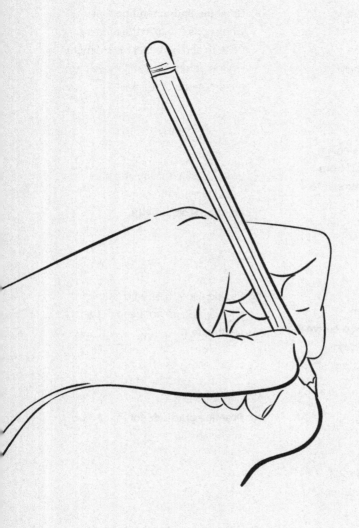

Daily exercises
for personal growth

~~~

To follow these exercises is crucial. They were designed specifically for your type and they all lead to personal growth and free you from unwanted habits. Sometimes these exercises can look pointless, but trust that they form a bigger picture. Our personalities also tend to resist personal growth as a way to protect what is familiar, but in order to expand our understanding of ourselves, we need to go beyond what we already know and there is always something new to be learned. Youaremoreworld team is together with you on this personal journey. Just remember that there are so many people travelling the same path as you and they can already confirm the benefits of all the exercises.

Take one exercise per day.

1.

Notice today when you start to feel that others have negative thoughts about you. Do you feel that they are criticizing or judging you? Observe how you automatically go into a defensive mode without checking with them what they truly meant? What actions can you take in order to clarify what their true intentions are?

Write your notes here

_____

_____

_____

_____

_____

_____

_____

_____

_____

_____

_____

_____

_____

_____

_____

_____

_____

_____

_____

_____

_____

Today let's be aware when you feel emotionally engaged in some situations and you try to add drama elements to them. Do you feel like you add a some personal interpretation in order to make those situations feel more alive? What do you truly want when you make situations more dramatic? What is deep inside you that you do not accept and express to others?

Write your notes here

3.

Allow yourself to observe the feeling that there is something missing in this moment. Even if it is hard to define what it is, take a pen and paper and try to write down all of the thoughts which are coming to you. What is missing? Where is this feeling located in your body? How does it serve you?

Write your notes here

4.

Be aware whenever you fall into your fantasy world. Notice when you create different stories, different situations which never happened in reality but which you have simply dreamed. Observe how deep you go into your imagination, to see how much of your experiences actually occurred in your life. While there is nothing wrong with living in a creative fantasy world, there is a very fine line where you start to enjoy that world more than the one you are living in. The more you embrace your fantasies, the less you keep yourself engaged in the real world in which you live. Try to remember the last few times when you spent a longer time in your fantasy world. Write them down and take some time to explore the thought - how did they benefit your soul?

Write your notes here

5.

Today, take one thing you always wanted to do but always found reasons not to do. Think about the first step you can take today to start, even if it does require some effort and planning. You are awesome, I am proud of you. Reward yourself with a treat for staying committed to your idea.

Write your notes here

6.

Set aside today to do an experiment. Every time you feel unpleasant or negative emotions about any situation, try to find a positive side to it. It is not an easy task, but it brings peace to your soul. After a day, write down your experience. Did you feel like you weren't being true to yourself when you tried to change your feelings to the positive? How often did you feel inner resistance?

Write your notes here

7.

Today take some time to observe your feelings. Notice how often you think that you are what you feel. Especially when those strong, powerful feelings move through your body, notice how you become what you feel. Whenever it happens, bring awareness to your breathing and try to separate yourself from what you feel. It does not define your personality. Feelings mirror your reaction to the situation and it is always important to notice them, but recognize how they are just representation of a specific moment and how quickly it passes. Allow yourself to observe and write down your thoughts on the topic: who am I without my feelings?

Write your notes here
_____
_____
_____
_____
_____
_____
_____
_____
_____
_____
_____
_____
_____
_____
_____
_____
_____
_____
_____
_____
_____

»»»

Today be aware of any time you imagine conversations inside your mind. Observe how you construct them while considering different scenarios. How often do you experience this process? What do you get from these conversations? Which part of your personality are you serving? Notice how unlikely it is for us to know what another might say in a moment and how little we can actually prepare. Allow yourself to bring all of your valuable experience into your daily conversations and to experience what is really happening in the present moment in your day to day situations.

Write your notes here

9.

Rate from 1 to 10 the love you feel toward yourself. What do you love yourself for? Can the opinions of others affect your own love for yourself? If yes, why?

Write your notes here

10.

Take some time today and write down 5 good qualities of each of your co-workers who you for some reason do not like. How often do you find yourself seeing others as boring or not interesting? How often do you reach conclusions about them before getting to know them better? How often do you come to the conclusion that someone is not worth your time but then after spending some time with them and getting to know them, you change your opinion? What is the true reason for you not being fond of all of those people? What is your judgement trying to protect you from?

Write your notes here

11.

Take some time today and write on these topics:

What is a unique person to me? How do I imagine that person would look? What personal qualities does he/she hold?

Once you finish writing, ask yourself - is this who I actually am or want to be but am not allowing myself to express? Would I agree with the statement that once a person allows himself to be who he really is, he becomes naturally unique, authentic?

Write your notes here

People of your type fear that if their emotions are not sufficiently intense, their creativity and even their identity will disappear. Take some time today and observe yourself during the day to see if you can feel this process of using your imagination to stir up how you feel. Pay attention to your fantasies, daydreams, and self-talk. What are they reinforcing? What purpose do they serve?

Write your notes here

13.

Practice gratitude this week. Take five minutes in the evening and think about all the things which have happened today. Find at least 10 things you can be grateful for. It is very important to notice things you can thank yourself for. Maybe you listened to a random stranger when he needed you. Maybe you did someone a favor even though you had a lot of work do. These are just a couple of examples. What is your list of what you are grateful for?

Write your notes here

14.

Take some time and observe yourself. Which qualities do you fantasize about having? Notice which of these qualities you might actually be able to develop. For example, it is true that music requires some talent, but none of that talent will be realized if you do not develop it through practice and discipline. Similarly, being in shape requires exercise and balanced diet. Also notice which qualities are unattainable; being taller or from a different background, for instance? What is it about these qualities that attracts you? Can you feel the self-rejection in wishing to be these things? Can you recognize the value in the qualities you do have?

Write your notes here

15.

Today observe your tendency to focus on your differences with other people. How does it affect your connection to others? How do you feel when you separate yourself from others? Does it prevent you from taking some actions, participating in some activities which could benefit your growth and expand your being?

Write your notes here

16.

Notice when you start to feel like you are losing your identity and personal „I". In which situations do you feel this way? What is this „You" who is disappearing at these times? Who do you see yourself become without it? Who is the one watching this process?

Write your notes here

17.

Your type has a tendency to have stormy conflicts with people and to then reconnect with them by making up. Notice your tendency to create drama in your primary relationships. What are you really frustrated about? What behavior are you trying to elicit from the other person? How close have you come to truly alienating people you love with this pattern?

Write your notes here

18.

Get reality checks from people when you are feeling that they are judging, criticizing, or rejecting you. Ask them to clarify what they meant, and allow for the possibility that they may be telling you exactly what they feel. Avoid „over interpreting" or "over reading" every gesture and comment that others are making. Chances are good that they are not scrutinizing you in this kind of detail. Notice your degree of interest in others and the nature of your comments and thoughts about them as well. Would you find this acceptable in them?

Write your notes here

*Notice when you are experiencing different feelings and how you consider some of them as „You"
and some you consider as „not you". How do you decide which feelings belong to which category?
How do you know that some feelings are not you even if you are the one who is noticing them? Write
down 10 emotions which exist in the world, but which are not part of your personality. Take some
time to observe them. Take one of them, close your eyes and feel the reason why are you having
hesitation about it. Once you are ready, move to the next one. Write down all of your insights.*

Write your notes here

20.

Notice when you feel like there is something wrong with you. How does this feeling prevent you from seeing the good personal qualities you already have? Who are you serving when you constantly remind yourself that there is something wrong with you? What if you would see that there is nothing wrong with you, who would you become? How does this feeling correlate with the situations you are experiencing? Are there some thoughts from the past which trigger this feeling?

Write your notes here

21.

What is your personal baseline mood most of the time? How do you react if you are spontaneously not in that mood? Notice any tendency to run a commentary on your feelings and experiences, as if asking yourself: what does this experience say about me? Every time you find yourself fantasizing, especially about potential romance or becoming your idealized self, you are moving deeper into the trance of Type four.

Write your notes here

Notice when and how you withdraw from people and events, making yourself an outsider when you do not have to be, not participating in social events when you could. Can you distinguish when this is a legitimate choice arrived at with equanimity and when it is an emotionally charged reaction that is probably the result of an old childhood issue? Can you stay with your reaction long enough (without acting it out) to see what is at the root of it?

Write your notes here

Become aware whenever you have the feeling that you want to be the only one for the person you care the most about. How much of your effort comes from the core of love and how much from the fear that if you don't put enough effort that you might not be the „only one" for them. Do you hold the belief that you can be better than the other people in your loved one's life? What criteria do you have in mind when you evaluate your actions? What do you feel when you consider that you are equal to everyone else?

Write your notes here

Notice when you feel like your identity changes every time different feelings arrive. It is a good place to start asking yourself some questions. Who am I if my identity can be changed so easily? What is the base of my personality which I already know that I am? Which of my beliefs cannot be changed by any situation? Can I imagine my identity without feelings? Who would I be if I wouldn't experience any feelings?

Write your notes here

25.

Today let's write all of the talents, skills and qualities that you have always dreamed about. After making your list, observe it. What stops you from actually developing these skills and qualities? Take the one thing from your list which means the most to you and promise yourself to commit to it. Are you truly ready to take daily steps required in order to own that dream? What is the first action you feel like taking toward it? Make a commitment to yourself that no matter what will happen today that you will take that step toward your dream. Whenever you are ready to take actions toward the other things, always come back to this list. Note that we recommend working on one or two things at a time as more than this could be overwhelming and you might end up not taking any actions at all.

Write your notes here

26.

Notice when you withdraw from the people you care about in a form of „hiding" with the intention for them to notice your action and to „find" you. What expectations do you have from the other person when you play this game? What conclusions have you already prepared if they do not notice your game? What one specific thing are you trying to get from the other person? Can you name which one thing you are asking from the other person when you choose to play this game? Would it bring more mutual understanding if you were to share directly with the person what your needs are and how they can know you better? Do people actually know what you are trying to say when you play this game?

Write your notes here

27.

Your type has a tendency to value others for how they look or for things they do. Every time you feel your attention drawn to judging others, try to find at least 2 things that you like about that person or what you could learn from him/her, and how the world benefits by them being here. Practice accepting others for who they are without trying to change them or devalue them in your mind.

Write your notes here

28.

Notice when you withdraw yourself from others in order to protect your feelings. How do you feel in that moment when you choose to disconnect yourself? How would you like this situation to be different? In what ways could you stay in that discomfort and expand your being? What if you wouldn't have to protect anything, how would you feel? How would you express yourself to others?

Write your notes here.

29.

When we forgive ourselves, this feeling awakens our inner peace. Allow yourself every day for a week to practice forgiveness. Try to spend at least a few minutes forgiving yourself for specific things, forgive the others who you feel hurt you. Write down how you feel after each practice. Do you feel lighter? Do you still have the same difficult feeling?

Write your notes here

Notice when you become involved in the feeling that there is something missing within you, your life or your relationships. How do you know that there is something missing? In which moment do you start having this feeling? When you experience this feeling, are you comparing your life with how it was and with what is no longer? Would you truly change the place where you are right now to where you were in the past? What do you have in this present moment that is so much more valuable than everything you had in the past? What actions do you need to take to fill the space that is missing in this present moment?

Write your notes here

31.

Notice how often you postpone your plans because you do not feel you are in the right mood, how sometimes you truly want to do something but you cannot overcome your moodiness. Take one simple step in the direction of realizing one of your plans and see how it is enough to just take one step and you already have a different energy flowing through you. Write three ways you think you could overcome your moodiness. My secret tip – do not even think that you are not in the mood, do not let your mind analyze it, instead just start!

Write your notes here

Let's take some time today and observe your emotions and feelings. Can you notice when they arrive? What situations give them space to be noticed by you? Have you noticed what effect they have on your personality? Where in your body do you experience your feelings? How do they change over time? Do your surroundings influence them? Do you have control of how they affect your inner world?

Write your notes here

33.

Take some time this week for an honest conversation with your parents. The best would be to speak with them in person but if you do not have an opportunity, then call or text them. Choose the method which serves both sides. Tell them what you are grateful for, share with them honestly what is happening at this stage in your life. Observe within yourself when you cannot or do not want to share one or other, these are likely the meaningful things which you need to share in order to be honest with them. Write down what happens inside you after the conversation.

Write your notes here

34.

Write down 20 things you love about yourself. Read them aloud to yourself, feel the heat which like a radiating energy moves through your body. Feel it. How often do you experience this energy during the day?

Write your notes here

35.

Meditation is a great way to feel the present moment. Take a 14-day challenge to find 15 minutes for meditation every day. Find a comfortable calm place, close your eyes and follow your breath. Feel how you inhale and exhale. If any thoughts come forth, do not push them away just transfer focus back on your breathing. Observe how the thoughts pass through you without staying too long when you do not engage them. After 14 days write down your thoughts, did the quality of your meditation change over time? Do you feel that it brings some value to you and that you would like to continue to do this?

Write your notes here

36.

Personal transformation begins with noticing your repeated patterns in everyday life. Remember, it's not about over-analyzing and changing every emotional state that produces transformation, but self-knowledge and awareness. Don't try to change your reactions today, it's enough to start to see them more clearly.

Write your notes here

Write down three things you would like to learn even though you may feel you are no good at doing them at this stage. Try to look into them and ask yourself - why did I not start to learn them up until this point? Is there perhaps some fear of failing preventing me?" Who is that inside you who feels shame if you try and do not succeed? Notice how this feeling prevents you from expressing yourself fully. Notice when, instead of taking the direct route, you are instead looking for the easiest steps and have a hope that one day things would be different and that you will have better conditions to act on.

Write your notes here

Today it's the day for self-love. What does it mean for you? Do you feel that you take enough time to take care of yourself and tell yourself how much you love this person looking at you in the mirror?

Write your notes here

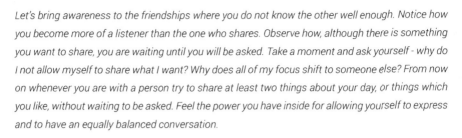

Let's bring awareness to the friendships where you do not know the other well enough. Notice how you become more of a listener than the one who shares. Observe how, although there is something you want to share, you are waiting until you will be asked. Take a moment and ask yourself - why do I not allow myself to share what I want? Why does all of my focus shift to someone else? From now on whenever you are with a person try to share at least two things about your day, or things which you like, without waiting to be asked. Feel the power you have inside for allowing yourself to express and to have an equally balanced conversation.

Write your notes here

_____

_____

_____

_____

_____

_____

_____

_____

_____

_____

_____

_____

_____

_____

_____

❝

To be yourself in a world that is constantly trying to make you something else is the greatest accomplishment.
Ralph Waldo Emerson

Today is a positive affirmation day. Choose one or two affirmations and repeat them in your mind or out loud throughout your day. Write down what shift of your mindset you may have noticed and which thoughts have appeared when you say the affirmations.

Write your notes here

AFFIRMATIONS:

I draw on my experiences to grow.
I choose to release the past.
I am in the present moment.
I transform pain into power.
I am more than my human experience.
I appreciate the beauty and goodness in life.
I am centered in my true essence.
I am anchored in my being.
I draw on my gifts to inspire the world.
I am happy to be me.
I am joyous in the present.
I have unique capabilities.
I practice equanimity.

Source: www.evelynlim.com

If you find it difficult working on your daily exercises by yourself, please join our community and discover the support it offers. Write us an email to learn more about programs that are available at this stage:
youaremoreworld@gmail.com

If you complete all of your daily exercises, please share your experience with us and be in the draw to win goods from our **Youaremoreworld shop.**

Notes

Notes

Notes

Accepting myself

Accepting all that I am

Making conscious choices

Letting go

Step 1

I accept that I allow my feelings to define who I am

I accept that I make my own value less by comparing myself with others, only recognising their positive traits

Authentic

Self- accepting

I accept that I choose to create drama in my relationship in order to intensify it

I accept that I choose to live in memories of the past rather than creating my future

Intuitive

When I accept both sides of my personality, my strengths gain even more power

I accept that it is hard for me to forgive others

Compassionate

Creative

I accept that occasionally I reduce the value of other people

I accept that I do not give others the opportunity to understand and to know me

Forgiving

Introspective

Expressive

Accepting myself

There is no greater gift that we can give ourselves than that of true acceptance of who we are, seeing our whole self with an open heart. This allows us a sense of curiosity and braveness to see our faults as well as our gifts without casting judgment on them, simply able to observe ourselves as we are. It is in these moments that we are able to feel the truth of our existence arising, understanding that who we are now has a long history. Through our lives we are touched by each of our experiences, which forms the understanding we have of the world and shapes the unique expression we bring to the world. Each of these qualities — those that form the uniqueness we bring to the world — was born with a purpose of supporting us during a specific period of our life; however, we often resist these qualities. Perhaps this resistance is because we want to be different, or because those in our surroundings don't approve of these qualities. Whatever the reason, we all respond to these unwanted qualities in the same way: we abandon them, ignoring them as though they are not a part of us, until they become our shadows, limiting us and preventing us from living the best life we are truly meant to live.

The first step on the journey of our own healing is to accept that there is nothing wrong with the qualities we have which we consider as negative; they all have a purpose to serve. As we move through different periods of our lives, we require different qualities, and these eventually form the bigger picture of who we are; so our only task for now is to **accept this variety of qualities without judgment.**

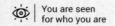
To start, **write a list of all of the qualities and traits** which are dominant to your personality that you consider to be negative. Make sure you add all of the qualities you can think of, especially those that you feel most uncomfortable about. Some examples of this could be: *sometimes I put a lot of effort into being seen as unique, to stand out from the crowd; or, I choose to live in memories of the past rather than creating my future.* Or you can simply write a quality, like being stubborn or often feeling jealous (you can find more examples in *picture 1*). We recommend being as specific as you can, remembering situations where you experienced the qualities on your list, for example: *I feel jealous when others are more successful than me.* You may want to use some of the new knowledge you have gained from this book to support you in writing this list. If you feel some resistance or hesitation toward certain qualities, add them to the list as well. Often the qualities that we strongly resist make up a shadow side of ourselves.

Once you have written the list of qualities, take some time to go over the examples and see if any of those qualities resonate with you. If so, add them to your list. When you are all done, move on to the second part of this exercise — "Accepting all that I am".

Intuitive

Creative

Authentic

Self- accepting

Compassionate

Forgiving

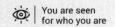

For this step, simply go through your list of descriptions of qualities one by one and add **"I accept that..."** before each description. Take time to sit with each quality to feel this acceptance. For example, *"I accept that sometimes I put a lot of effort into being seen as unique, to stand out from the crowd. And now I am conscious of it." "I accept that I experience jealousy when others are more successful than me."* etc.

Accepting all that I am

Bringing our shadow side to the light

I accept that *sometimes I put a lot of effort into being seen as unique, to stand out from the crowd. And now I am conscious of it.*

Step 2

Making conscious choices

Once you have taken time to accept your different qualities, you may notice that some of them contradict what you currently value in your life and that some of the qualities are no longer valuable for you. This is a very natural state for us as humans because it is in our nature to constantly grow and change. The ability to look into our hearts with honesty and to see our whole selves, including all of our practiced personality traits, allows us to experience a sense of empowerment and the inner strength to act on it.

In order to experience the change which we are seeking, it is important to embrace the positive aspects of the quality in order to align it with our true values. Use the following exercise to expand the positive aspects of your qualities:

I might .... but I choose to...

Take some time to fill-in the boxes below based on the qualities you discovered in the first step of this exercise.

I might ..... *be hard on others by not forgiving them,*
but I choose to ..... *look with my heart and to see that everyone is doing the best that they can. I now choose to love and support them rather than judging them and living in a feeling of guilt.*

I might ....

....

but I choose to...

....

....

....

I might ....

....

but I choose to...

....

....

....

I might ....

....

but I choose to...

....

....

....

I might ....

....

but I choose to...

....

....

....

I might ....

....

but I choose to...

....

....

....

I might ....

....

but I choose to...

....

....

....

I might ....

....

but I choose to ....

....

....

....

I might ....

....

but I choose to ....

....

....

....

I might ....

....

but I choose to ....

....

....

....

Healing myself

Identifying with your future self

Healing yourself

Revealing yourself

Meditation

Affirmations for aligning with your true self

Within a year from today I will:

I commit to doing the following to create the quality life I deserve to live:

_____

_____

_____

_____

_____

_____

_____

_____

_____

_____

_____

_____

_____

_____

_____

_____

_____

_____

_____

_____

_____

_____

_____

Identifying with your future self

The knowledge of Enneagram is not about simply putting us into a box; it is a valuable tool that can show us that we are living a limited version of ourselves and that we have the potential to be much more — that there is a way out of that box. The moment we accept what we learn about the qualities of our dominant type, we gain the freedom to expand our qualities and to become whatever we want. We will still hold the basis of our dominant type, as this is our gift which supports our soul on this journey. However, as we appreciate ourselves as we are, we are able to see which traits are limiting us and integrate more positive qualities to support us in realizing our dreams. Take some time today to consider **who you would like to become by the end of this year.** How would you like your life to look? Which qualities would you like to have? What goals would you have accomplished? You might also consider your relationship, health and finances etc. Be as specific as you can and take your time in writing it all down. If you aren't able to finish this exercise in one sitting, simply return to it when you feel ready to explore your expanded future.

Once you have written all of your wishes, take this piece of paper and put it somewhere visible where you will see it often. Take 5 minutes every day to imagine how it will feel to live this life that you want to live. The more time you take to imagine your future self, the more information you are providing for your subconscious to direct your actions in your desired direction. Sooner than you might expect you will notice that you are already acting with the traits you had on your wish list. For example, if you write on your list that you would like to be an engaging person when you are with others, you will notice that you begin to experience more frequent possibilities for you to express this quality. If, on your list, you had a specific workplace noted, you will find yourself guided to more direct actions toward realizing this.

In our lives, we always have the choice, to either be directed by unconscious actions or to be proactive in learning about ourselves and building the life that we truly want to live. This leads us to realize that there is much more to Enneagram than simply being one of the types; it can guide us to be more and to live honestly through each new moment that unfolds for us.

Healing yourself [4]

The things to which we are exposed every day become our reality. When practiced often, the sentences below have the potential to bring you into greater alignment with your heart.

Affirmation:
I am connected
to love.

Confession:
I am conscious of
compassionate
belonging.

Healing:
Maybe there is nothing wrong with me.
Maybe others do understand me and are supporting me.
Maybe I am not the only one who feels this way.

"Because true belonging only happens when we present our authentic, imperfect selves to the world, our sense of belonging can never be greater than our level of self-acceptance."

Brené Brown

Revealing yourself

The following questions have been created uniquely for your type, offering new perspectives for you to consider about yourself. Take some time to give thought to each question individually, and write your thoughts below.

In which situations do **I feel misunderstood?**

_____

_____

In what ways do I put my attention toward **what is missing?**

_____

_____

How do I **undervalue things** of a boring or mundane nature?

_____

_____

Why is it so important for me **to be unique and different** from others?

_____

_____

When do I experience **envy, jealousy or longing?**

_____

_____

_____

_____

_____

Meditation
for your daily practise

 It takes 5- 10 min.

Find a peaceful, secure place,
close your eyes and repeat the sentences below:

Notice how, with each sentence, your heart begins
to open up, allowing you to feel stronger in your
own body. Feel how this process awakens the
true understanding of yourself, which has always
existed within.

May I see myself.
May I know myself.
May I love myself.

By Christopher L. Heuertz

Practicing self-acceptance and unravelling our beliefs helps us to see ourselves more fully. This awakens a new sense of knowing within us, despite the occasional thoughts that make us feel smaller. Consider the following sentences and how they represent a deep inner truth you have always known:

When I free myself
I would gain the knowledge that:

feelings do not define my personality;

I use my feelings only to express myself;

I open myself to other people and the world;

I draw on my experience in my efforts to grow;

I enjoy the beauty of life, friends and myself;

I love and appreciate myself;

I am free from my past;

I will bring to life something beautiful.

Source: Don Richard Riso, Enneagram Transformations.
Houghton Mifflin Company, 1993, 129 pages.

Additional exercises
supporting your personal growth

———

How I want my future to look

*Making balanced decisions based on
the 9 perspectives of Enneagram*

*Expanding my beliefs with
Byron Katie's 4 question technique*

> *"The goal is not to be better than the other man, but your previous self."*
>
> *Dalai Lama XIV*

How I want my future to look

As humans, it is common for us to focus specifically on one single thing when it comes to planning (improve a relationship, change career, etc.). One of the keys for true happiness is to keep balance across all of the important areas of our life. Take some time to think about the areas listed below, and consider what would you like to achieve in each within the coming year. Write down all of the ideas that come to you. Take some time to act toward your priorities, as this can add great value to your overall well-being.

Personal development

For example: read three books about self-love.

For example: spend more time with my mother.

Relationships

Career

For example: ask for X responsibility that would help toward moving into a team leader position.

For example: take a day trip to X town.

Leisure

For example: change the tiles in my bathroom.

Home

For example: transfer 10% from my salary into a savings account.

Finances

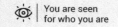
Making balanced decisions
based on the 9 perspectives of Enneagram

Making decisions can be an overwhelming experience, especially when we are not sure which of the options would be the right one for the outcome we are seeking. Take some time to review a situation in your life that requires a decision by using the 9 questions offered below, each of which represents one of the 9 Enneagram types:

1. What exactly do I not like in this situation?

2. For whom will it be beneficial if I change this situation?

3. Which end-result am I reaching for, and when does it have to be done?

4. How can I solve this situation by using my creativity?

5. What information am I still missing?

6. What kind of danger could I face while I am solving this situation?

7. What are possible solutions for this situation?

8. What is an action plan?

9. How will I reward myself when I finish?

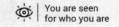
Expanding my beliefs
with Byron Katie's 4 question technique

Byron Katie's work has had an incredible impact on many people, helping them to better understand their thoughts and to increase their well-being. She created a 4-question system, where by going through each question, we can discover how many of our thoughts are based on false stories which repeatedly cause stress and anxiety. Once we become comfortable questioning our thoughts, we can use this exercise to work with our underlying beliefs which are no longer relevant for our reality.

We added this technique to the book alongside the knowledge of Enneagram, because we can see how much it can help those who want to take their path of inner work into their own hands.

Byron Katie's 4-question technique:

1. *Is it true?*
2. *Can you absolutely know that it's true?*
3. *How do you react, what happens, when you believe that thought?*
4. *Who would you be without that thought?*

Underlying belief:

"I feel that most of the time others are better than me."

STEP 1

Let's question this belief using Byron Katie's four-question technique.

1. Is it true that others are better than you?

   - *Yes*

2. Can you be absolutely sure that others are better than you?

   - *No*

3. How do you feel or react when you think that others are better than you?

   - *I feel very low self-value. I feel I am not worthy to do some things. I want to disconnect and be by myself.*

4. Who would you be without this thought that others are better than you?

   - *I do not know. Maybe I would feel that I am equal even if I do not have some qualities others have. And I can develop the qualities I want.*

STEP 2

Looking at the belief from three different perspectives.

Turn it around to yourself
I am enough as I am.

Turn it around to the others
I am equal to others.

Turn it around to the opposite
Others are not better than me.

Note: the answers are included simply as an example. Follow your own thoughts and discover the answers which are true for you.

If you would like further support in understanding this technique, please see Byron Katie's website or her many valuable books.

Bibliography

1. Baron Renee Baron and Wagele Elizabeth. The Enneagram made easy: Discover the 9 types of people. New York, 1994.

2. Ford, Debbie. The Dark Side of the Light Chasers. USA, 1998.

3. Heuertz, Christopher L. The Enneagram of Belonging: A Compassionate Journey of Self —Acceptance. Grand Rapids, MI: Zondervan, 2020.

4. Riso, Don Richard, and Russ Hudson. The Wisdom of the Enneagram: The Complete Guide to Psychological and Spiritual Growth for the Nine Personality Types. New York: Bantam, 1999.

5. "Revealing yourself" source of information: www.enneagramworldwide.com

Recommended books

1. *You Can Heal Your Life* by Louise L. Hay

2. *The Power of Now* by Eckhart Tolle

3. *Rising Strong* by Brené Brown

4. *The Dance of Connection* by Harriet Lerner

5. *Intuition* by Osho

6. *The Dark Side of the Light Chasers* by Ford Debbie

7. *The Artist's Way* by Julia Cameron

8. *The Power of Positive Thinking* by Norman Vincent Peale

9. *Big Magic: Creative living beyond fear* by Elizabeth Gilbert

10. *The Mindful Path to Self Compassion* by Christopher Germer

11. *Love yourself like your life depends on it* by Kamal Ravikant

12. *Creative visualization* by Shakti Gawain

13. *Quiet: The power of introverts in a world that can't stop talking* by Susan Cain

14. *Sacred Contracts* by Caroline Myss

15. *Sacred Woman: A Guide to Healing the Feminine Body, Mind, and Spirit* by Queen Afua

16. *The Wisdom of the Enneagram* by Don Richard Riso and Russ Hudson

17. *The Enneagram of Belonging* by Christopher L. Heuertz

18. *The Enneagram made easy* by Renee Baron & Elizabeth Wagele

19. *The Untethered Soul: The Journey Beyond Yourself* by Michael Alan Singer

20. *Why Won't You Apologize?* Harriet Lerner

Who are we?

Youaremoreworld was built on an idea to encourage others to their own personal growth. Our mission is to awaken curiosity in people, helping them to learn more about themselves, questioning their beliefs - especially the ones which no longer serve them. Encouraging their sense of freedom in order to allow them to live what truly matters to them. For all of us, our origin is the same, having been conditioned and trained by our surroundings, however, we all also equally have the opportunity to reconnect to our true selves and to release what's no longer needed. Enneagram is an incredibly valuable resource to begin this process. Here at *Youaremoreworld*, we use the knowledge of Enneagram as the basis for our work, helping people to uncover the "persona" which they have formed in order to interact with daily life.

The Enneagram exercise book you have in your hands is one of a collection of nine books, each serving a different Enneagram type. We hope that this book will serve its purpose and assist you in your further journey of self-discovery.

We are constantly expanding the horizons here at *Youaremoreworld*, seeking new ways in which we can serve the greater community. If you liked our book, please join us at **www.youaremoreworld.com** and stay up to date with the work we are doing. The greatest gift we can receive is your feedback to help us to continually improve.

Thank you for being a part of our community, we will see you out there in the wilderness, where your heart directs the footsteps of your unique soul.

With Gratitude,
Viltare and Simona

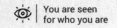
Contact us:

✉ youaremoreworld@gmail.com

✐ www.youaremoreworld.com

ⓕ youaremore_world

⦿ youaremore_world

Read
with us

Learn
with us

Shop
with us

Books
in this collection

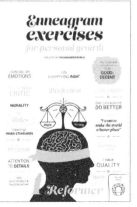

Acknowledgements

Only with the help of others we can reach the stars

Thank you to our teachers Don Richard Riso and Russ Hudson who compiled all of the knowledge of Enneagram and inspired many people around the world to look into their hearts and unlock their own potential. They were also a great inspiration for us to publish these exercise books for anyone who chooses Enneagram as a tool for their own personal growth.

We would love to give credit to Christopher L. Heuertz for his talent of approaching the Enneagram with great compassion, encouraging others to accept the full spectrum of their personality (including the sides which may be viewed as incompetence or limitation). You will find his meditations, affirmations and confessions which, when practiced daily, can heal the heart.

Also, we would like to acknowledge Jack Labanauskas for his constant work in keeping the Enneagram community alive and connected through his "Enneagram monthly" magazine which can be joined by visiting:
http://www.enneagram-monthly.com/

Our superstar Matthew Fulton, who reviewed each page with the most sincere eye, making sure that every word would be written in a correct and most understandable way. You are part of Youaremoreworld family, thank you for your hard work.

We are very grateful for our parents: Viltare's (Leonora and Virginijus, and the best grandma in the world Antanina) and Simona's (Lijana and Rimgaudas) for giving us the freedom to explore this life and for providing support in all of its possible forms. We are also grateful for our partners Hanno and Dan for providing us with inspiration and encouragement through all of the steps required to publish all our work. And lastly our Enneagram teacher Nadezda Doronina-Koltan, who opened the door for us to discover this great wisdom and to guide us to the master class of understanding.

*I now open myself to others
and to the world around me*

Made in the USA
Las Vegas, NV
17 February 2023

67719802R00077